Naughty OR *nice* COUPONS

SOURCEBOOKS CASABLANCA™
AN IMPRINT OF SOURCEBOOKS, INC.®
NAPERVILLE, ILLINOIS

Published by Sourcebooks, Inc.
P.O. Box 4410, Naperville, Illinois 60567-4410
(630) 961-3900
FAX: (630) 961-2168
www.sourcebooks.com

Printed and bound in the United States of America
DR 10 9 8 7

This coupon is good for a big serving of

your favorite chocolate dessert—mousse, devil's food cake,

hot fudge sundae, anything you want.

Naughty

This coupon is good for an evening of delicious fun with chocolate sauce—no bowls, no spoons, just you and me!

This coupon is good for an afternoon of

reading romantic poetry to one another.

Naughty

With this coupon, we each pick our favorite racy

passage from a book and read it to one another.

This coupon is good for one super-sweet voicemail

from me in which I will list all of my favorite things about you.

Naughty

This coupon is good for one sexy daytime

phone call/voicemail in which I will list all the

things I plan to do to you when we get home.

This coupon is good for a big bowl of chocolate kisses—
with a kiss from me for every one you unwrap!

Naughty

With this coupon I promise to

kiss you anywhere you want me to.

This coupon is good for one super-snuggle hour.

Present this coupon and I will spend one hour

giving you incredible pleasure.

Redeem this coupon for a day in the country,

complete with a walk through the forest and a picnic lunch.

Naughty

With this coupon, I will make love to you on a mountaintop or under a tree, where we can feel the breeze on our skin and the sun on our faces.

When this coupon is presented, I will drop whatever

I am doing and give you a soothing back massage for thirty minutes.

Present this coupon and I will drop everything and make love to you.

This is an all-powerful VETO coupon. Present this coupon

and you can change plans at the last minute, without warning!

Present this coupon when you'd like to be helpless and let me

have my way with you for a specified period of time.

nice

This coupon is good for a relaxing bubble bath. I'll prepare the bath, and supply you with wine and fruit to make it a peaceful time.

Let's take a shower together with scented soap and loofah toys.

This coupon is good for one game of miniature golf...

and an ice cream treat afterward.

This coupon is good for one game of strip poker—winner takes all.

Present this coupon and receive one romantic dinner,

complete with candlelight and music.

Naughty

This coupon is redeemable for a candlelight
dinner (at home) wearing as little as possible and sitting
so we can touch—I'll hand-feed you dessert.

nice

Let's spend an evening together exploring downtown,

including dinner and window-shopping.

This coupon is good for a lingerie shopping spree...

as long as we go shopping together!

This coupon is good for a romantic nighttime picnic under the stars.

Naughty

You and me, a beautiful night, and a double

sleeping bag—I'll bring the hot toddies.

Present this coupon and I will drop everything

and write you a note telling you how much I love you.

Present this coupon and I will put into writing exactly

what I like best about our lovemaking—in detail.

This coupon entitles you to one shopping trip

at the jewelry store of your choice.

This coupon entitles you to one shopping

trip at the sex store of your choice.

nice

This coupon entitles you to call me and

have me bring you a coffee, a cookie, or whatever

you need to make your day better.

Naughty

This coupon means I'm on call for a
quickie whenever you need it today.

This coupon entitles you to one picnic at the beach of your choice.

Let's go skinny-dipping!

nice

This coupon entitles you to a historical tour of

your choice, or a visit to a museum of your choice,

so we can get ideas for role-playing that night.

This coupon entitles the bearer to an evening of dress-up.

Upon presentation of this coupon, I will hold you

until we can feel our hearts beating together.

Upon presentation of this coupon, I will grab you and kiss you until you are gasping for air.

This coupon entitles you to breakfast in bed—and I'll clean up.

This coupon entitles you to one good morning _____!

This coupon is good for lunch at a nice restaurant, whenever you like.

When you present this coupon, we will make love

at a time and place of your choosing.

When you present this coupon, I'll tell you

something you always wanted to know about my childhood.

Present this coupon and we'll live out your fantasy—no limits.

This coupon is redeemable for one movie that will make

you laugh out loud, as much popcorn as you

can eat, and candy of your choice.

Naughty

With this coupon I will take you to a risqué movie

and sit in the back row with you so we can fool around.

Present this coupon and I will wear the outfit you like best on me.